ART FROM THE
SECOND WORLD WAR

A BOOK OF POSTCARDS

Pomegranate

PORTLAND, OREGON

Pomegranate Communications, Inc.
19018 NE Portal Way, Portland OR 97230
800 227 1428; www.pomegranate.com

Pomegranate Europe Ltd.
Unit 1, Heathcote Business Centre, Hurlbutt Road
Warwick, Warwickshire CV34 6TD, UK
[+44] 0 1926 430111; sales@pomeurope.co.uk

ISBN 978-0-7649-6692-7
Pomegranate Catalog No. AA804

Pomegranate publishes books of postcards on a wide range of subjects.
Please contact the publisher for more information.

Cover designed by Tristen Jackman
Printed in Korea
22 21 20 19 18 17 16 15 14   10 9 8 7 6 5 4 3 2 1

To facilitate detachment of the postcards from this book, fold each card along its perforation line before tearing.

DURING THE SECOND WORLD WAR, at the instigation of National Gallery Director Sir Kenneth Clark, the Ministry of Information established the War Artists Advisory Committee (WAAC) as the government's official war art program. Throughout the war, art exhibitions were organized in Britain and the United States to raise morale and promote Britain's image abroad. By the end of the war the WAAC had collected 5,570 works produced by more than four hundred artists. After the committee's demise in 1945, the Imperial War Museum (IWM) took over administration of the scheme, particularly as portraits were still being produced in the postwar years. More than 3,250 original oil paintings, drawings, and a number of sculptures from this collection are now in IWM's care. It is the most complete and representative example of WAAC material worldwide and a unique visual collection of great significance—not only is it a record of the war efforts by Britain and Allied countries, the artworks also resonate with personal experiences and stories.

ART FROM THE **SECOND WORLD WAR**

Keith Henderson (1883–1982)
A North-east Coast Aerodrome, 1940
Oil on canvas, 69.8 x 90.1 cm (27½ x 35½ in.)

© IWM (Art.IWM ART LD 257)

WWW.POMEGRANATE.COM

800 227 1428

Pomegranate

ART FROM THE **SECOND WORLD WAR**

Eric Ravilious (1903–1942)
A Warship in Dock, 1940
Pencil and watercolor on paper,
44.1 x 58.7 cm (17⅜ x 23⅛ in.)

© IWM (Art.IWM ART LD 70)

800 227 1428 WWW.POMEGRANATE.COM

Pomegranate

IWM
WAR
IMPERIAL WAR MUSEUMS

ART FROM THE **SECOND WORLD WAR**

William Roberts (1895–1980)
Women Railway Porters in Wartime
Watercolor and pencil crayon on paper,
38.4 x 55.9 cm (15⅛ x 22 in.)

© IWM (Art.IWM ART LD 1701)

WWW.POMEGRANATE.COM

800 227 1428

Pomegranate

ART FROM THE **SECOND WORLD WAR**

Walter Bayes (1869–1956)
*Battle of Britain: Parachutists from an enemy aircraft brought
down in an apparent attempt to bomb Buckingham Palace*, 1942
Oil on canvas, 119 x 140.9 cm (46⅞ x 55½ in.)

© IWM (Art.IWM ART LD 2514)

WWW.POMEGRANATE.COM

800 227 1428

Pomegranate

IWM
IMPERIAL WAR MUSEUMS

ART FROM THE **SECOND WORLD WAR**

Walter Thomas Monnington (1902–1976)
Southern England, 1944. Spitfires Attacking Flying-Bombs, 1944
Oil on canvas, 105.4 x 143.3 cm (41½ x 56 7⁄16 in.)

© IWM (Art.IWM ART LD 4589)

WWW.POMEGRANATE.COM

800 227 1428

Pomegranate

ART FROM THE **SECOND WORLD WAR**

Roland Vivian Pitchforth (1895–1982)
The Chamber, The House of Commons, 1942
Watercolor and wax crayon on paper,
77.1 x 111 cm (30⅜ x 43¹¹⁄₁₆ in.)

© IWM (Art.IWM ART LD 1581)

ART FROM THE **SECOND WORLD WAR**

Charles Ernest Cundall (1890–1971)
Motor Launches, Dartmouth, 1940
Oil on canvas, 65.7 x 124.4 cm (25⅞ x 49 in.)

© IWM (Art.IWM ART LD 1215)

WWW.POMEGRANATE.COM

800.227.1428

Pomegranate

ART FROM THE SECOND WORLD WAR

Eric Kennington (1888–1960)
Parachutes, 1941
Pastel on paper, 73.6 x 53.3 cm (29 x 21 in.)

© IWM (Art.IWM ART LD 1259)

WWW.POMEGRANATE.COM

800 227 1428

Pomegranate

ART FROM THE **SECOND WORLD WAR**

Keith Henderson (1883–1982)
Wings Over Scotland, 1940
Oil on canvas, 50.8 x 60.9 cm (20 x 24 in.)

© IWM (Art.IWM ART LD 634)

WWW.POMEGRANATE.COM

800 227 1428

Pomegranate

ART FROM THE **SECOND WORLD WAR**

Roy Anthony Nockolds (1911–1979)
Stalking the Night Raider, 1941
Oil on canvas, 63.5 x 76.2 cm (25 x 30 in.)

© IWM (Art.IWM ART LD 1150)

ART FROM THE **SECOND WORLD WAR**

Keith Henderson (1883–1982)
An Air Gunner in Action Turret: Night, 1940
Oil on canvas, 76.2 x 101.9 cm (30 x 40⅛ in.)

© IWM (Art.IWM ART LD 633)

ART FROM THE **SECOND WORLD WAR**

John Edgar Platt (1886–1967)
The Quick Turn-round, 1943
Oil on canvas, 89 x 78.8 cm (35$\frac{1}{16}$ x 31 in.)

© IWM (Art.IWM ART LD 3827)

IWM
WAR
IMPERIAL MUSEUMS

ART FROM THE **SECOND WORLD WAR**

John Armstrong (1893–1973)
Building Mosquitoes, 1943
Tempera on panel, 55.8 x 81.2 cm (22 x 32 in.)

© IWM (Art.IWM ART LD 3359)

WWW.POMEGRANATE.COM

800 227 1428

Pomegranate

ART FROM THE **SECOND WORLD WAR**

Charles Pears (1873–1958)
A German Searchlight across the English Channel, 1942
Oil on canvas, 81.2 x 127 cm (32 x 50 in.)

© IWM (Art.IWM ART LD 1916)

ART FROM THE **SECOND WORLD WAR**

Laurence Stephen Lowry (1887–1976)
Going to Work, 1943
Oil on canvas, 45.7 x 60.9 cm (18 x 24 in.)

© IWM (Art.IWM ART LD 3074)

WWW.POMEGRANATE.COM

800 227 1428

Pomegranate

ART FROM THE **SECOND WORLD WAR**

Walter Thomas Monnington (1902–1976)
Fighter Affiliation: Halifax and Hurricane aircraft
co-operating in action, 1943
Oil on canvas, 46.3 x 41.2 cm (18¼ x 16¼ in.)

© IWM (Art.IWM ART LD 3769)

WWW.POMEGRANATE.COM

800 227 1428

Pomegranate

ART FROM THE **SECOND WORLD WAR**

John Armstrong (1893–1973)
Building Planes, 1940
Gouache on paper, 37.1 x 54.2 cm (14⅝ x 21⁵⁄₁₆ in.)

© IWM (Art.IWM ART LD 6390)

ART FROM THE **SECOND WORLD WAR**

Charles Ginner (1878–1952)
Building a Battleship, 1940
Oil on canvas, 83.8 x 60.9 cm (33 x 24 in.)

© IWM (Art.IWM ART LD 252)

WWW.POMEGRANATE.COM

800 227 1428

Pomegranate

ART FROM THE **SECOND WORLD WAR**

Charles Ernest Cundall (1890–1971)
Battle of Britain Anniversary, 1943:
RAF Parade at Buckingham Palace, 1943
Oil on canvas, 96.5 x 152.4 cm (38 x 60 in.)

WWW.POMEGRANATE.COM

800 227 1428

ART FROM THE **SECOND WORLD WAR**

C. Eliot Hodgkin (1905–1987)
The Haberdashers' Hall, 8th May 1945, 1945
Tempera on panel, 29.2 x 36.8 cm (11½ x 14½ in.)

© IWM (Art.IWM ART LD 5311)

ART FROM THE **SECOND WORLD WAR**

Laura Knight (1877–1970)
A Balloon Site, Coventry, 1943
Oil on canvas, 102.5 x 127 cm (40⅜ x 50 in.)

© IWM (Art.IWM ART LD 2750)

WWW.POMEGRANATE.COM

800 227 1428

Pomegranate

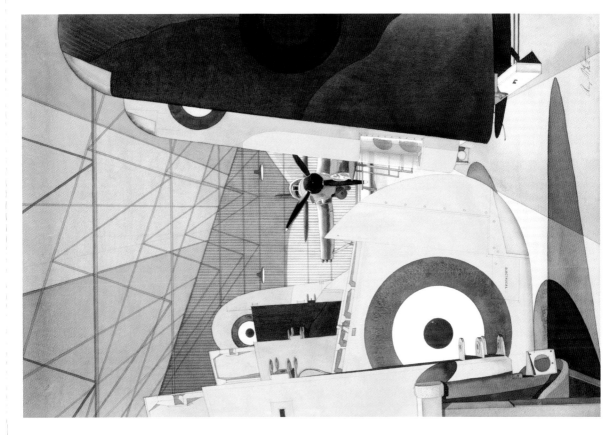

ART FROM THE **SECOND WORLD WAR**

Raymond McGrath (1903–1977)
Training – Aircraft Under Construction, 1940
Watercolor on paper, 55.7 x 37.9 cm (21$\frac{15}{16}$ x 14$\frac{15}{16}$)

© IWM (Art.IWM ART LD 65)

800 227 1428   WWW.POMEGRANATE.COM

ART FROM THE **SECOND WORLD WAR**

Frank Mason (1876–1965)
*The Model-Maker's Shop: Directorate of Camouflage
(Naval Section) Leamington Spa*, 1943
Oil on panel, 41.2 x 50.8 cm (16¼ x 20 in.)

© IWM (Art.IWM ART LD 2755)

800 227 1428   WWW.POMEGRANATE.COM

Pomegranate

ART FROM THE **SECOND WORLD WAR**

Walter Thomas Monnington (1902–1976)
Tempests Attacking Flying-bombs, 1944
Oil on canvas, 90.1 x 114.3 cm (35½ x 45 in.)

© IWM (Art.IWM ART LD 4588)

WWW.POMEGRANATE.COM

800 227 1428

Pomegranate

ART FROM THE **SECOND WORLD WAR**

Henry Carr (1894–1970)
Mosquito Nets, 1943
Oil on canvas, 73.6 x 104.1 cm (29 x 41 in.)

© IWM (Art.IWM ART LD 3070)

WWW.POMEGRANATE.COM

800 227 1428

ART FROM THE **SECOND WORLD WAR**

Albert Richards (1919–1945)
The Drop, 1944
Oil on panel, 54.9 x 75.2 cm (21⅝ x 29⅝ in.)

800 227 1428 WWW.POMEGRANATE.COM

Pomegranate

ART FROM THE **SECOND WORLD WAR**

Frank Wootton (1914–1998)
Rocket-firing Typhoons at the Falaise Gap, Normandy, 1944, 1944
Oil on canvas, 105.4 x 151.1 cm (41½ x 59½ in.)

© IWM (Art.IWM ART LD 4756)

ART FROM THE **SECOND WORLD WAR**

Charles Ernest Cundall (1890–1971)
The Exterior of St Paul's Cathedral on Thanksgiving Day,
13th May 1945, 1945
Oil on canvas, 121.9 x 182.8 cm (48 x 72 in.)

© IWM (Art.IWM ART LD 5773)

WWW.POMEGRANATE.COM

800 227 1428

Pomegranate

ART FROM THE **SECOND WORLD WAR**

Frederick William Elwell (1870–1958)
A Munitions Factory, 1944
Oil on canvas, 62.8 x 75.5 cm (24¾ x 29¾ in.)

© IWM (Art.IWM ART LD 4908)

WWW.POMEGRANATE.COM

800 227 1428

Pomegranate